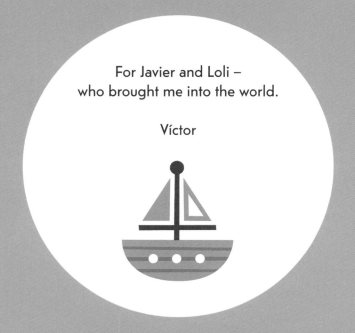

For Javier and Loli –
who brought me into the world.

Víctor

© for the Spanish original edition: 2018, Mosquito Books, Barcelona
www.mosquitobooksbarcelona.com
© for the illustrations: 2018, Victor Medina
© for the text: 2018, Mia Cassany
© for the English edition: 2018, Prestel Verlag, Munich · London · New York
A member of Verlagsgruppe Random House GmbH
Neumarkter Strasse 28 · 81673 Munich

Prestel Publishing Ltd.
14-17 Wells Street
London W1T 3PD

Prestel Publishing
900 Broadway, Suite 603
New York, NY 10003

Library of Congress Control Number: 2017964103
A CIP catalogue record for this book is available from the British Library.

Translated by Paul Kelly
Copyediting: Brad Finger
Production management: Astrid Wedemeyer
Typesetting: Meike Sellier, Eching
Printing and binding: TBB, a.s.
Paper: Tauro

Verlagsgruppe Random House FSC® N001967

Printed in Slovakia

ISBN 978-3-7913-7355-3
www.prestel.com

GREAT PORTS OF THE WORLD

FROM NEW YORK TO HONG KONG

· VÍCTOR MEDINA ·

Text by Mia Cassany

PRESTEL

Munich · London · New York

It's more than likely that you have seen a port, or maybe you live near a harbor or have a boat moored in one.

A port is a very special place. There is a secret hidden in every corner; every unseen spot is hiding something; every nook and cranny can reveal fabulous stories and exciting adventures.

Harbors are attractive in a mysterious kind of way, and there is something going on around the clock. A port never sleeps. Its hustle and bustle never die down in the daytime or night.

Harbors come in every shape and size, but they all have the same function: they are a kind of hotel for ships, a shelter for the biggest of ocean liners and the smallest of sailboats. Some ports shelter boats completely covered by hand-sewn fishing nets. In other ports, cranes hoist huge containers filled with goods onto cargo ships. These vessels will transport the goods all over the world and from one place to another.

The oldest ports were once a starting point for the adventures of sailors, merchants, and pirates. Incredible and notorious tales were reported on their jetties and their piers. Nowadays, however, modern harbors may remind you of huge space ships. They are equipped with the most complex technologies for controlling thousands of ships, passengers, and containers with absolute precision.

Every port has its own character. They welcome us on behalf of their city. Ports are always receiving new goods and new visitors. They are wardens of the seas and tireless workers, yet compared with other parts of their cities – the cathedrals and skyscrapers – ports get little attention from tourists.

Without wishing to, I found myself falling in love with ports and with their wonderful lighthouses! In the course of this book, I would like to show you some of the most exciting secrets and oddities of famous ports around the world. Would you like to join me in this adventure?

All aboard!

The Port of New York is one of America's busiest when it comes to the volume of passenger and container traffic. It is located at the mouth of the Hudson River in Upper New York Bay. The approach to the harbor from the ocean is dominated by the Statue of Liberty, which welcomes all inbound shipping. Can you spot Lady Liberty in this picture?

An important fact: The Statue of Liberty was a gift from France to the citizens of New York in 1875. It honored the centenary (or 100-year anniversary) of the independence of the United States. However, the statue wasn't actually completed until 1886.

The Port of Hong Kong is Asia's gateway to the world. Every day of the year, and that includes public holidays, more than 1,200 ships enter or leave here, transporting either goods or passengers.

A statistic: The port's annual record of container movement is about 25 million, which means a container is being loaded or unloaded every single second.

The Port of Hamburg was built in the deep waters of the River Elbe and lies about 115 kilometers (70 miles) from the river's estuary. It is Germany's largest access to the sea. Due to its location and special features, Hamburg is particularly well suited for the transportation of cargo. Hardly any other port in the world transfers as many containers as Hamburg does.

Here is a remarkable but true fact: Hamburg's port was founded more than 800 years ago.

St. Petersburg, city of the Czars, was the capital of imperial Russia. What an elegant city this is! Its canals, palaces and churches leave people in awe. St. Petersburg's harbor is located at the mouth of the River Neva, and it services shipping from the Baltic.

Here is a bit of trivia: In less than one century, the city changed its name three times. Originally called St. Petersburg, the city became Petrograd in 1914 and then Leningrad in 1924. Finally, in 1991, the Russian people gave the city its original name back!

The Port of London is truly ancient and stretches along the banks of the River Thames in southern England. During the 18th and 19th centuries, a great deal of industry settled there, causing layers of smog to cover the city from hundreds of industrial chimneys.

Here is a strange thing: Like many historic ports on rivers, the Port of London is not located in an enclosed area. Instead, it consists of dozens of jetties,

The great, primeval forests of Africa, South America, and other continents provide the Earth with the oxygen we need to breathe. But that is not the only thing these places offer. Many of the people who live there are from cultures that have dwelled in the forest for thousands of years, cultures that have much to teach us about preserving the rainforest environment. Rivers provide the most important means of transport...

GATI 2

and communication here. The small harbors and jetties along the riverside are where not only goods are exchanged but also where news is passed along.
Here are some statistics: The River Congo is 4,700 kilometers (2,920 miles) long and flows right through the African rain forest. It's hard to imagine how big it really is.
The jungle around the Congo Basin alone spans six countries and, after the Amazon in South America, it is the second largest rain forest in the world.

The ports at the poles, where temperatures can drop to -40°C or lower, serve neither tourists nor container ships. They were created so researchers and scientists could travel there and study the climate, landscape, and wildlife. In the Arctic regions around the North Pole, native peoples called Inuits can live in extremely harsh conditions. However, no humans live permanently in Antarctica around the South Pole.

There is a little white lie in this picture: Polar bears and penguins don't really live together. Penguins live in Antarctica and polar bears live in the Arctic.

For the ancient Egyptians, the River Nile was a source of wealth and abundance. Almost all ancient Egyptian cities and temples were located close to the river. The yearly floods made the fields lying close to the riverside fertile and guaranteed rich harvests.

A good thing to know: Egypt's most important port is in the Mediterranean city of Alexandria. It contains countless little ports and jetties.

On the shores of the Mediterranean, in such places as the Côte d'Azur in France, there are elegant, sunny, welcoming harbors in picturesque locations. Every year they receive thousands of holiday boats, yachts, and cruise ships from all over the world.

A point of interest: Saint-Tropez is among the most famous towns in the Côte d'Azur and one of the areas that welcomes the most tourists, who arrive mainly by sea.

Surfers enjoy dozens of small tourist harbors on the coastlines of Hawaii. With a lush volcanic landscape as a backdrop, these beachy places are ideal for catching waves. Look out, though, as the waters are teeming with sharks!

An important note: Even though it is an archipelago (or group of islands) that lies thousands of miles away in the middle of the Pacific Ocean, Hawaii is part of the United States.

Amsterdam also has an important port. However, visitors are much more interested in the many waterways, or canals, that crisscross the city and contain endless numbers of jetties, small docks, piers, and boats.

Here is a little fact: It is thought that more than 12,000 bicycles fall into the canals each year, which is not really very many if you consider that there are 880,000 of them in Amsterdam!

KADE 8

Barcelona is one of the largest ports in the Mediterranean and one of the biggest cruise ship ports in the world. Every year, 2.5 million tourists disembark from these ocean liners, which are more like floating towns.

A few statistics about this port: Large cruise ships are more than 300 meters (980 feet long, and some tower up to 10 stories high and transport up to 5,000 people, including the crew. Their populations are larger than many neighborhoods in Barcelona.

TIC
TAC

TIC
TAC

MOLO 5

Dozens of 'gondolieri' in their gondolas wait for passengers near St. Mark's Square in order to row them through the canals of Venice. This ancient, watery city has hundreds of small piers for its gondolas, its vaporetti (this is what the local water buses are called), and its water taxis.

A few more details: A real Venetian gondola is 11 meters (36 feet) in length and is steered using just a single oar at the stern, where the gondolier stands upright. Sadly, these beautiful boats are not as common in Venice as they used to be.

The Portuguese city of Porto is famous for its wines of the same name. Delicious port wines are shipped around the world, but this would not be possible without Porto's magnificent harbor on the River Douro and its estuary on the Atlantic Ocean.

More trivia: Both the name of the city and the wine actually mean 'harbor' or 'port', a fact that underlines the importance of Porto's shipping industry.

DOCA 23

Japanese ports have always been a major driver of trade and a boost to their country's economy. Traditional Asian fishing boats are called 'junks'. They have large sails and a flat bottom.

Now for a bit of history: Junks originally came from China. These wooden ships sailed from port to port for more than 2,000 years and were the main vehicles for transporting goods among the various peoples there.

Gigantic ports can handle millions of passengers and an incredible movement of goods. However, there are also smaller, quieter ports and harbors, where just a few fishing vessels are anchored before setting off on their journey every day. These fishing harbors blend into their towns just like in any other neighborhood.

Which port is your favorite?

A Journey Around the World!

Do you recognize these pictures?

NEW YORK

New York is located on the East coast of North America.

The Statue of Liberty is the city's most famous landmark.

The Brooklyn Bridge crosses the East River and connects the boroughs (or city districts) of Manhattan and Brooklyn.

The Chrysler Building, one of the city's most famous skyscrapers, was completed in 1930 and is 319 meters (1,046 feet) high.

The Empire State Building, constructed between 1930 and 1931, used to be the city's tallest building at a height of 381 meters (1,250 feet).

Hong Kong

The huge city of Hong Kong lies on the south coast of China.

Countless container ships transport goods from here to the whole world. The containers are loaded by cranes. It's hard to imagine how every container reaches the right destination!

Hamburg

Hamburg is located in the north of Germany.

The Elbphilharmonie (Elbe Philharmonic Hall), which can be seen from quite a distance away, is the city's newly built concert hall.

The water level tower on the landing stages indicates the elevation of the water.

Saint Petersburg

The big picture of St. Petersburg shows the city as it used to look.

The pretty building with the colorful onion-shaped domes is a Russian orthodox church.

Further to the right, the dome of St. Isaac's Cathedral towers above all the other buildings.

London

The English capital of today looks a lot different from the picture in this book. London now has many skyscrapers, and the air is no longer thick with smog. But it still rains quite often.

Typical sights in London are the red double-decker buses and 'Big Ben', the famous bell tower in the Palace of Westminster.

Congo

The River Congo flows right through the middle of Africa.

Rhinos and crocodiles live along its banks.

What other animals can you find here?

The Arctic and Antarctica

The Arctic lies in the northernmost end of the world, while the Antarctic lies in the southernmost end. Yet both have the same bitterly cold climate. Very few creatures are able to survive in these places.

Penguins only live in the South Pole, where they rear their young in the icy landscape.

Polar bears only live around the North Pole.

Egypt

Egypt lies in the north of Africa on the Mediterranean. More than 5,000 years ago, a sophisticated civilization arose there.

The ancient Egyptians built huge pyramids here.

The great Sphinx – a sculpture of a lioness with a human head – stands guard next to the pyramids of Giza.

Saint-Tropez

The Côte d'Azur is a popular holiday destination in the south of France, and Saint-Tropez is one of its best known resorts.

The city's beauty has made it a rendezvous point for artists and actors since the 1950s.

Hawaii

Hawaii is an archipelago in the middle of the Pacific. Its capital is Honolulu.

Hawaii is a true holiday paradise and especially popular with surfers.

Amsterdam

Amsterdam is the capital city of the Netherlands. The North Sea Canal connects the city to the North Sea.

Barcelona

The capital of Spain's Catalonian region is also the country's second largest city.

The renowned church of Sagrada Família designed by architect Antoni Gaudí, has been under construction since 1882, and it's still not complete! Its towers look somewhat like rock formations.

Venice

Venice, Italy, is not just famous for its gondolas, but also for its historic Rialto Bridge.

More than 500 years ago, Venice was one of the world's most important trading cities, with ships bringing valuable supplies into Europe from the East. A large part of the city is built on stilts in the middle of the Venetian Lagoon.

Japan

Japan is an East Asian country and part of a group of islands alongside China and Korea.

Do you see the banners that resemble carp fish? They are typical for this country.

Porto

The city lies in Portugal's north, on the Atlantic coast at the Douro estuary.

In this city, you can see the famous Ponte de Dom Luis iron bridge above the river, the cable car gondolas, and the old-fashioned trams.